THOMPSON®

CHAIN-REFERENCE®
SERMON NOTEBOOK

THOMPSON®

CHAIN-REFERENCE®

SERMON NOTEBOOK

Save and Organize Your Thompson
Chain-Reference Bible Studies

Randy A. Brown

ZONDERVAN®

ZONDERVAN

Thompson® Chain-Reference® Sermon Notebook
Copyright © 2024 by Zondervan

Published in Grand Rapids, Michigan, by Zondervan. Zondervan is a registered trademark of The Zondervan Corporation, L.L.C., a wholly owned subsidiary of HarperCollins Christian Publishing, Inc.

Requests for information should be addressed to customercare@harpercollins.com.

Zondervan titles may be purchased in bulk for educational, business, fundraising, or sales promotional use. For information, please email SpecialMarkets@Zondervan.com.

ISBN 978-0-310-15958-2 (softcover)

Any internet addresses (websites, blogs, etc.) and telephone numbers in this book are offered as a resource. They are not intended in any way to be or imply an endorsement by Zondervan, nor does Zondervan vouch for the content of these sites and numbers for the life of this book.

Cover design: LUCAS Art & Design
Interior design: Kait Lamphere

Printed in India

24 25 26 27 28 29 30 31 32 33 /BPI/ 14 13 12 11 10 9 8 7 6 5 4 3 2 1

HOW TO STUDY THE BIBLE WITH THE THOMPSON CHAIN-REFERENCE BIBLE

The *Thompson Chain-Reference Bible* (TCR) is a topical chain reference system with indexes and tools connecting 8,000 topics and 100,000 chain references. These tools form the Thompson Study System, which allows Bible readers to interpret Scripture with Scripture. The TCR tools are excellent for saving time in sermon outline preparation. Below is a summary of the tools available in the TCR, how to use them to study the Bible, and tips on converting Bible study notes into sermon outlines.

TOPICS AND CHAIN REFERENCES IN THE MARGINS

The margins of the TCR look different from other reference Bibles. Topics for each verse are listed in the margins. They identify major themes in the text and show the topical numbers, topic names, and the reference to the next verse in each topical chain. Most verses include multiple topics with a topic number, topic name, and chain reference for each topic. With the Thompson Study System, the reader follows a topic through the Bible one verse at a time. Using it helps the Bible teacher or preacher build biblical sermons. The reader can also use the topic numbers to find more verses on any topic in the Numerical Index of Topics.

ALPHABETICAL INDEX OF TOPICS

Many of the tools and guides for deeper Bible study are in the back of the TCR. The Alphabetical Index of Topics is one of the most important reference tools. Similar to a concordance, the Alphabetical Index is where to look to find any topic in the TCR listed alphabetically. This index includes topic names and topic numbers for subjects, names, places, and events. The Alphabetical Index is the best place to look when studying a topic. Each entry includes the topic number, leading the preacher to the Numerical Index and other tools.

NUMERICAL INDEX OF TOPICS

Having found the topic number in the Alphabetical Index, use the Numerical Index to see all the topics with their primary verses printed in full. The user can read the prominent verses in this index or turn to the verses in the biblical text to see them in context. Most topics in the Numerical Index are grouped into larger topics, so the surrounding topics are related. Subtopics, suggested topics, and related topics are listed under their topic numbers. The surrounding topics and related topics expand theme study, helping the preacher add more detail to the sermon if needed.

TOPICAL TREASURY

The Topical Treasury is a noteworthy feature of the TCR for Bible study leaders and pastors. It helps Bible preachers and teachers because it offers a list of sermon and lesson starters. It provides topics in many categories and suggests topics appropriate for several types of meetings. Use this feature of the TCR to find a topic and its corresponding topic number. Then look up that topic in the Numerical Index.

More Bible Study Helps in the TCR

The back of the TCR contains even more tools. It is worth highlighting a few more that provide information, more topic lists, life overviews of the most prominent biblical characters, and details about notable events in biblical history.

The Condensed Outline of the Bible gives one-to-two sentence overviews of each biblical book. The outline divides the books into the Old Testament and the New Testament and then into sections within the testaments. The Old Testament sections include the Pentateuch, historical books, major prophets, and minor prophets. The New Testament sections include the Gospels, Acts, epistles of Paul, general epistles, and Revelation.

Book Introductions are found at the beginning of each book of the Bible. They list the prominent people, key words, main chains, a detailed outline called a synopsis, and key verses. They provide insights into each book of the Bible.

The Bible Character Studies are biographies and outline studies of the most prominent biblical characters from the Old Testament. These studies provide information on a character's family, early and later life developments, and key events that make the character noteworthy. Additionally, the Bible Character Studies section features tables with information about the Apostles and the messianic prophecies.

Moreover, the Bible Harmonies and Illustrated Studies section pulls together great information in the Bible, the early church, and discipleship resources. To name just a few, this section includes maps, lists, life overviews, Outline History of the Early Church,

Distance in Miles between Old Testament Cities, Topical Treasury, Christian Worker's Texts, Memory Verses, Aids to Memorization, Places of Religious Worship and Religious Leaders, Hebrew Times, Seasons, and Festivals, and more.

All the TCR tools work well together to make the TCR a great single resource to assist Bible teachers and preachers in studying the Bible and developing teaching and preaching materials. This sermon notebook was designed to work with those tools. Now that we've seen how to study the Bible using the Thompson Study System, let's see how to use this sermon notebook to organize those notes and use them as a guide for writing teaching material and sermon outlines.

USE THE TCR TOOLS FOR ALL PREACHING STYLES

The TCR excels as a resource for preparing sermons in multiple styles, such as topical, biographical, and expository. The TCR helps the preacher develop strong points, examples, and illustrations. We will briefly analyze the various styles and see how the TCR helps with each style.

TOPICAL SERMONS

The TCR provides a detailed overview of any topic and the context of each verse, saving time in topical research. Search the Alphabetical Index for the topic number. Turn to the topic number in the Numerical Index to see the verses for that topic. Browse the verses, turn to a verse in the biblical text, follow the chain through the Scriptures, and examine the related and suggested topics.

Analyze the passages, make notes of the topics and verses to use in the sermon, and create a sermon outline from those notes.

EXPOSITORY SERMONS

The TCR's tools provide a starting point for generating sermon ideas and content for those sermons. Book Introductions and the Condense

Outline of the Bible provide information on the main themes, characters, key events, and more. The topics in the margins provide insights into the major themes of every passage. They help preach through any book, chapter, or passage of the Bible.

Analyze the introductions, outlines, and marginal topics. Make notes of the points to use in the sermon and create a sermon outline from those notes.

BIOGRAPHICAL SERMONS

The Bible Character Studies tool provides information on the key biblical characters with detailed information including outlines, charts, and a synopsis that identifies key events and key points.

Analyze the character information and make notes of the character traits, events, and history to use in the sermon. Create a sermon outline from those notes.

TCR SERMON
PREPARATION TIPS

The Thompson Study System removes the time-consuming research needed for sermon prep, allowing the preacher to focus on the message. To help ease the process further, here are a few tips for sermon preparation with the *Thompson Chain-Reference Study Bible.*

- Utilize all the TCR's tools for in-depth study.
- Read the passages in context.
- Write down notes as you study.
- Record the main topics and passages.
- Record the main points.
- Note the supporting topics and their references.
- Cite the supporting passages to build supporting points.
- Note the recommended topics for further study.
- Use only the TCR Sermon Notebook fields needed.
- Write the sermon outline from these notes.
- Use only the notes needed.
- Refer to the notes if another point is needed during the sermon.
- Use multiple pages per sermon if needed.

HOW TO USE THIS
SERMON NOTEBOOK

The TCR Sermon Notebook is an exciting and useful tool that guides the user and simplifies the TCR's tools for teaching and sermon prep. This section discusses the pages found in the TCR sermon notebook and provides information on how to use them.

PAGES

In the front are several pages with an explanation of how to use the TCR for sermon prep with examples.

The main body of this TCR Sermon Notebook includes a two-page spread. The page on the left includes fields to enter the sermon study notes. This helps keep topics, verses, points, and additional thoughts together. Use them to build a sermon outline, manuscript, bullet points, or any other favorite sermon-writing method, on the lined page on the right. These pages are numbered so the preacher can use the page numbers for reference or to create an index in the back.

The fields to create the sermon notes include:

Title—this is the title of the sermon.
Scripture—this is the main passage or verse to focus on.
Topics and Chains—these are the topic names and numbers
to use.

Main Topic—this is the main topic of the sermon. It should include the topic name and number.

Main Verses—these are the main verses to use.

Main Points—these are the main points to cover.

Supporting Topic—this is the first supporting topic or thought to support the main topic.

Verses—these are the verses related to the first supporting topic.

Points—these are the main points of the first supporting topic.

Supporting Topic—this is the second supporting topic or thought to support the main topic.

Verses—these are the verses related to the second supporting topic.

Points—these are the main points of the second supporting topic.

Additional Thoughts—this field is where the preacher can record any additional thoughts or notes to help develop the sermon. It could include an illustration, a name, a book, a location, or anything the preacher wants to remember.

The page on the right only includes ruled lines. This is so the preacher can write the sermon in their preferred method. Add the sermon title and main reference at the top of the page, and then add the outline, bullet points, and other information on the ruled lines. Preachers can also use this page for additional notes when using multiple pages to create a larger sermon.

Additionally, there are several pages in the back the preacher can use to create an index of their sermons. Index them by topic number, topic name, sermon name, date, and so on.

EXAMPLES

This section shows how to develop a sermon using the TCR and the TCR Sermon Notebook. It will show how to develop both an expository sermon and a topical sermon.

Expository Sermon

For expository sermons, the preacher should explore the marginal topics of the passage they want to cover. Decide on a main point from those topics. Use the verse for that topic or the entire passage as the primary verse or verses. Use the topics in the margins for the main points, highlighting the most prominent topics as supporting topics. Add the relevant verses and points for each supporting topic. Finally, add additional thoughts in the last field.

Here is an example of how these fields can be used for an expository sermon.

Notes

Title: *How We Hear and Respond to God's Word*

Scripture: *Lk 8:4–15*

Topics and Chains: *Spiritual Sowing, 3424; Careless Hearing, 943; Hardness (1), 2716; Instability (2), 3444; Emotional Hearers, 4029; Worldly Care, 3021; Spiritual Receptivity, 2960; God's Word Seed, 429*

Main Topic: *The Parable of the Sower*

Main Verses: *Lk 8:11–15*

Main Points: *Some on the path hear, but the devil takes it away. Some receive it with joy, but they are not grounded. Some hear but are choked by life's worries. Some have a good heart and retain it.*

Supporting Topic: *God's Word Is the Seed.*

Verses: *Lk 8:11*

Points: *God's Word is the seed we sow, but not everyone will accept it.*

Supporting Topic: *Satan's Work 3151*

Verses: *Lk 8:12*

Points: *The devil fights all hearers.*

Additional Thoughts: *Strive to recognize each type of hearer and work with them to help them stay on the right path.*

Use all the above information (that is written on the left page) to develop the outline on the page on the right.

Sermon Outline

Here is an example of how the notes in the fields can be used to create an expository sermon outline. The preacher can use the ruled lines on the right page to write the sermon in their preferred method. The expository sermon could follow a structure like this one:

Title and Reference: *How We Hear and Respond to God's Word—Lk 8:4–15*
  I. *The Parable of the Sower shows several types of hearers.*
    A. *We are to sow the Word of God to help others grow.*
    B. *Some will be careless in their hearing.*
    C. *Some will have a hardness of heart.*
    D. *Some have instability in their lives.*
    E. *Some are emotional hearers.*
    F. *Some care too much about worldly things.*
    G. *Some are open to hearing God's Word and will receive it.*
  II. *Jesus Explains the Parable*
    A. *Some on the path hear, but the devil takes it away.*
    B. *Some receive it with joy, but they're not grounded.*
    C. *Some hear but are choked by life's worries.*
    D. *Some have a good heart and retain it.*
 III. *God's Word Is the Seed—Lk 8:11*
    A. *God's Word is the seed we sow.*
    B. *Not everyone will accept God's Word.*
 IV. *Satan Works to Keep Us From—Lk 8:12*
    A. *The devil fights all hearers.*
  V. *Closing Thought*
    A. *Strive to recognize each type of hearer and work with them*
      to help them stay on the right path.

Topical Sermon

For topical sermons, or sermons that focus on themes, the preacher could find the topic in the Alphabetical Index, Topical Treasury, or similar lists, and turn to the topic number in the Numerical Index to see the Scripture references.

Here is an example using the topic of the *Word of God Is Inspired*, topic number 417. This topic includes twelve primary verses, seventeen secondary verses, and one additional subject. For supporting topics, the preacher could use the topics that fall under the same heading in the *Numerical Index: The Bible, The Word of God* (topics 414–445).

Notes

Title: *The Inspiration of God's Word*

Scripture: *2Ti 3:16*

Topics and Chains: *417, Word of God (M. Word Inspired)*

Main Topic: *The Bible is the inspired Word of God.*

Main Verses: *2Ti 3:16; 2Pe 1:21*

Main Points: *God inspired the biblical authors as they wrote, making the Bible "God-breathed."*

Supporting Topic: *We are to study the Word of God, topic 428.*

Verses: *Dt 17:19; Isa 8:20, 34:18; Jn 5:39; Ac 17:11.*

Points: *Every Christian must study the Scriptures.*

Supporting Topic: *The Bible is useful for teaching, topic 431.*

Verses: *Dt 11:19*

Points: *We should use the Bible to teach and lead others. It is our authority.*

Additional Thoughts: *Studying and cherishing the Word of God should be part of our daily walk with God. Drive this point home and encourage everyone to read and study the Bible daily.*

Sermon Outline

Here is an example of how the notes in the fields can be used to create a topical sermon outline. The preacher can use the ruled lines on the right page to write the sermon in their preferred method. The outline could look like this:

I. Title and Reference: *The Inspiration of God's Word*
   A. *If the Bible is the Word of God, we would expect it to identify itself as the Word of God.*

B. The Bible does identify itself as the Word of God.
    1. 2Ti 3:16
    2. 2Pe 1:21
C. The Bible also gives us examples of how God's Word is inspired.
    1. Jer 36:2
    2. Ac 1:6
II. We are to study the Word of God.
  A. We must study the book God gave us.
  B. The Bible itself tells us to study the Bible.
    1. Dt 17:19
    2. Isa 8:20
    3. Isa 34:18
    4. Jn 5:39
    5. Ac 17:11
III. The Bible is our authority.
  A. We are to teach it, even in our homes.
    1. Dt 11:19
IV. Ending
  A. Reiterate that the Bible is the Word of God, and it is crucial to our walk with God.
  B. We should teach it to our children.
  C. We should live by it.
    1. Reread the original verse, 2Ti 3:16.

THOMPSON

CHAIN-REFERENCE
SERMON NOTEBOOK

SERMON NOTES

Title: ....

Scripture: ....

Topics and Chains: ....

....

....

....

Main Topic: ....

Main Verses: ....

....

Main Points: ....

....

....

....

Supporting Topic: ....

Verses: ....

....

Points: ....

....

....

....

Supporting Topic: ....

Verses: ....

....

Points: ....

....

....

....

Additional Thoughts: ....

....

....

....

....

SERMON OUTLINE/NOTES

Title and Reference: ....

....

....

....

....

....

....

....

....

....

....

....

....

....

....

....

....

....

....

....

....

....

....

....

....

....

....

....

....

....

....

....

SERMON NOTES

Title: ....

Scripture: ....

Topics and Chains: ....

....

....

....

Main Topic: ....

Main Verses: ....

....

Main Points: ....

....

....

....

Supporting Topic: ....

Verses: ....

....

Points: ....

....

....

....

Supporting Topic: ....

Verses: ....

....

Points: ....

....

....

....

Additional Thoughts: ....

....

....

....

....

SERMON OUTLINE/NOTES

Title and Reference: ....

....

....

....

....

....

....

....

....

....

....

....

....

....

....

....

....

....

....

....

....

....

....

....

....

....

....

....

....

SERMON NOTES

Title: ....

Scripture: ....

Topics and Chains: ....

....

....

....

Main Topic: ....

Main Verses: ....

....

Main Points: ....

....

....

....

Supporting Topic: ....

Verses: ....

....

Points: ....

....

....

....

Supporting Topic: ....

Verses: ....

....

Points: ....

....

....

....

Additional Thoughts: ....

....

....

....

....

SERMON OUTLINE/NOTES

Title and Reference: ....

....

....

....

....

....

....

....

....

....

....

....

....

....

....

....

....

....

....

....

....

....

....

....

....

....

....

....

....

....

....

....

....

SERMON NOTES

Title: ....

Scripture: ....

Topics and Chains: ....

....

....

....

Main Topic: ....

Main Verses: ....

....

Main Points: ....

....

....

....

Supporting Topic: ....

Verses: ....

....

Points: ....

....

....

....

Supporting Topic: ....

Verses: ....

....

Points: ....

....

....

....

Additional Thoughts: ....

....

....

....

SERMON OUTLINE/NOTES

Title and Reference: ....

....

....

....

....

....

....

....

....

....

....

....

....

....

....

....

....

....

....

....

....

....

....

....

....

....

....

....

....

....

....

....

SERMON NOTES

Title: ....

Scripture: ....

Topics and Chains: ....

....

....

....

Main Topic: ....

Main Verses: ....

....

Main Points: ....

....

....

....

Supporting Topic: ....

Verses: ....

....

Points: ....

....

....

....

Supporting Topic: ....

Verses: ....

....

Points: ....

....

....

....

Additional Thoughts: ....

....

....

....

....

SERMON OUTLINE/NOTES

Title and Reference: ....

....

....

....

....

....

....

....

....

....

....

....

....

....

....

....

....

....

....

....

....

....

....

....

....

....

....

....

....

....

....

....

....

SERMON NOTES

Title: ....

Scripture: ....

Topics and Chains: ....

....

....

....

Main Topic: ....

Main Verses: ....

....

Main Points: ....

....

....

....

Supporting Topic: ....

Verses: ....

....

Points: ....

....

....

....

Supporting Topic: ....

Verses: ....

....

Points: ....

....

....

....

Additional Thoughts: ....

....

....

....

....

SERMON OUTLINE/NOTES

Title and Reference: ....

....

....

....

....

....

....

....

....

....

....

....

....

....

....

....

....

....

....

....

....

....

....

....

....

....

....

....

....

....

....

....

....

SERMON NOTES

Title: ....

Scripture: ....

Topics and Chains: ....

....

....

....

Main Topic: ....

Main Verses: ....

....

Main Points: ....

....

....

....

Supporting Topic: ....

Verses: ....

....

Points: ....

....

....

....

Supporting Topic: ....

Verses: ....

....

Points: ....

....

....

....

Additional Thoughts: ....

....

....

....

....

SERMON OUTLINE/NOTES

Title and Reference: ....

....

....

....

....

....

....

....

....

....

....

....

....

....

....

....

....

....

....

....

....

....

....

....

....

....

....

....

....

....

....

....

SERMON NOTES

Title: ....

Scripture: ....

Topics and Chains: ....

....

....

Main Topic: ....

Main Verses: ....

....

Main Points: ....

....

....

....

Supporting Topic: ....

Verses: ....

....

Points: ....

....

....

....

Supporting Topic: ....

Verses: ....

....

Points: ....

....

....

....

Additional Thoughts: ....

....

....

....

....

SERMON OUTLINE/NOTES

Title and Reference: ....

....

....

....

....

....

....

....

....

....

....

....

....

....

....

....

....

....

....

....

....

....

....

....

....

....

....

....

....

....

Sermon Notes

Title: ....

Scripture: ....

Topics and Chains: ....

....

....

....

Main Topic: ....

Main Verses: ....

....

Main Points: ....

....

....

....

Supporting Topic: ....

Verses: ....

....

Points: ....

....

....

....

Supporting Topic: ....

Verses: ....

....

Points: ....

....

....

....

Additional Thoughts: ....

....

....

....

....

SERMON OUTLINE/NOTES

Title and Reference: ....

....

....

....

....

....

....

....

....

....

....

....

....

....

....

....

....

....

....

....

....

....

....

....

....

....

....

....

....

....

....

....

Sermon Notes

Title: ....

Scripture: ....

Topics and Chains: ....

....

....

Main Topic: ....

Main Verses: ....

....

Main Points: ....

....

....

....

Supporting Topic: ....

Verses: ....

....

Points: ....

....

....

....

Supporting Topic: ....

Verses: ....

....

Points: ....

....

....

....

Additional Thoughts: ....

....

....

....

....

SERMON OUTLINE/NOTES

Title and Reference: ....

....

....

....

....

....

....

....

....

....

....

....

....

....

....

....

....

....

....

....

....

....

....

....

....

....

....

....

....

....

....

....

....

....

....

Sermon Notes

Title: ....

Scripture: ....

Topics and Chains: ....

....

....

....

Main Topic: ....

Main Verses: ....

....

Main Points: ....

....

....

....

Supporting Topic: ....

Verses: ....

....

Points: ....

....

....

....

Supporting Topic: ....

Verses: ....

....

Points: ....

....

....

....

Additional Thoughts: ....

....

....

....

....

SERMON OUTLINE/NOTES

Title and Reference: ....

....

....

....

....

....

....

....

....

....

....

....

....

....

....

....

....

....

....

....

....

....

....

....

....

....

....

....

....

....

....

....

....

Sermon Notes

Title: ....

Scripture: ....

Topics and Chains: ....

....

....

....

Main Topic: ....

Main Verses: ....

Main Points: ....

....

....

....

Supporting Topic: ....

Verses: ....

....

Points: ....

....

....

....

Supporting Topic: ....

Verses: ....

....

Points: ....

....

....

....

Additional Thoughts: ....

....

....

....

....

SERMON OUTLINE/NOTES

Title and Reference: ....

....

....

....

....

....

....

....

....

....

....

....

....

....

....

....

....

....

....

....

....

....

....

....

....

....

....

....

....

....

....

....

....

....

....

....

SERMON NOTES

Title: ....

Scripture: ....

Topics and Chains: ....

....

....

....

Main Topic: ....

Main Verses: ....

....

Main Points: ....

....

....

....

Supporting Topic: ....

Verses: ....

....

Points: ....

....

....

....

Supporting Topic: ....

Verses: ....

....

Points: ....

....

....

....

Additional Thoughts: ....

....

....

....

SERMON OUTLINE/NOTES

Title and Reference: ....

SERMON NOTES

Title: ....

Scripture: ....

Topics and Chains: ....

....

....

Main Topic: ....

Main Verses: ....

....

Main Points: ....

....

....

....

Supporting Topic: ....

Verses: ....

....

Points: ....

....

....

....

Supporting Topic: ....

Verses: ....

....

Points: ....

....

....

....

Additional Thoughts: ....

....

....

....

....

SERMON OUTLINE/NOTES

Title and Reference: ....

....

....

....

....

....

....

....

....

....

....

....

....

....

....

....

....

....

....

....

....

....

....

....

....

....

....

....

....

....

....

....

....

SERMON NOTES

Title: ....

Scripture: ....

Topics and Chains: ....

....

....

....

Main Topic: ....

Main Verses: ....

....

Main Points: ....

....

....

....

Supporting Topic: ....

Verses: ....

....

Points: ....

....

....

....

Supporting Topic: ....

Verses: ....

....

Points: ....

....

....

....

Additional Thoughts: ....

....

....

....

....

SERMON OUTLINE/NOTES

Title and Reference: ....

....

....

....

....

....

....

....

....

....

....

....

....

....

....

....

....

....

....

....

....

....

....

....

....

....

....

....

....

....

....

....

SERMON NOTES

Title: ....

Scripture: ....

Topics and Chains: ....

....

....

....

Main Topic: ....

Main Verses: ....

....

Main Points: ....

....

....

....

Supporting Topic: ....

Verses: ....

....

Points: ....

....

....

....

Supporting Topic: ....

Verses: ....

....

Points: ....

....

....

....

Additional Thoughts: ....

....

....

....

SERMON OUTLINE/NOTES

Title and Reference: ....

....

....

....

....

....

....

....

....

....

....

....

....

....

....

....

....

....

....

....

....

....

....

....

....

....

....

....

....

....

....

....

SERMON NOTES

Title: ....

Scripture: ....

Topics and Chains: ....

....

....

....

Main Topic: ....

Main Verses: ....

....

Main Points: ....

....

....

....

Supporting Topic: ....

Verses: ....

....

Points: ....

....

....

....

Supporting Topic: ....

Verses: ....

....

Points: ....

....

....

....

Additional Thoughts: ....

....

....

....

Sermon Outline/Notes

Title and Reference: ....
....
....
....
....
....
....
....
....
....
....
....
....
....
....
....
....
....
....
....
....
....
....
....
....
....
....
....
....
....
....
....
....

Sermon Notes

Title: ....

Scripture: ....

Topics and Chains: ....

....

....

....

Main Topic: ....

Main Verses: ....

....

Main Points: ....

....

....

....

Supporting Topic: ....

Verses: ....

....

Points: ....

....

....

....

Supporting Topic: ....

Verses: ....

....

Points: ....

....

....

....

Additional Thoughts: ....

....

....

....

....

SERMON OUTLINE/NOTES

Title and Reference: ....

....

....

....

....

....

....

....

....

....

....

....

....

....

....

....

....

....

....

....

....

....

....

....

....

....

....

....

....

....

....

....

....

....

....

....

SERMON NOTES

Title: ....

Scripture: ....

Topics and Chains: ....

....

....

....

Main Topic: ....

Main Verses: ....

....

Main Points: ....

....

....

....

Supporting Topic: ....

Verses: ....

....

Points: ....

....

....

....

Supporting Topic: ....

Verses: ....

....

Points: ....

....

....

....

Additional Thoughts: ....

....

....

....

SERMON OUTLINE/NOTES

Title and Reference: ....

SERMON NOTES

Title: ....

Scripture: ....

Topics and Chains: ....

....

....

....

Main Topic: ....

Main Verses: ....

....

Main Points: ....

....

....

....

Supporting Topic: ....

Verses: ....

....

Points: ....

....

....

....

Supporting Topic: ....

Verses: ....

....

Points: ....

....

....

....

Additional Thoughts: ....

....

....

....

....

SERMON OUTLINE/NOTES

Title and Reference: ....

....

....

....

....

....

....

....

....

....

....

....

....

....

....

....

....

....

....

....

....

....

....

....

....

....

....

....

....

....

....

....

....

....

SERMON NOTES

Title: ....

Scripture: ....

Topics and Chains: ....

....

....

....

Main Topic: ....

Main Verses: ....

....

Main Points: ....

....

....

....

Supporting Topic: ....

Verses: ....

....

Points: ....

....

....

....

Supporting Topic: ....

Verses: ....

....

Points: ....

....

....

....

Additional Thoughts: ....

....

....

....

....

SERMON OUTLINE/NOTES

Title and Reference: ....

....

....

....

....

....

....

....

....

....

....

....

....

....

....

....

....

....

....

....

....

....

....

....

....

....

....

....

....

....

....

....

....

SERMON NOTES

Title: ....

Scripture: ....

Topics and Chains: ....

....

....

....

Main Topic: ....

Main Verses: ....

....

Main Points: ....

....

....

....

Supporting Topic: ....

Verses: ....

....

Points: ....

....

....

....

Supporting Topic: ....

Verses: ....

....

Points: ....

....

....

....

Additional Thoughts: ....

....

....

....

....

SERMON OUTLINE/NOTES

Title and Reference: ....

....

....

....

....

....

....

....

....

....

....

....

....

....

....

....

....

....

....

....

....

....

....

....

....

....

....

....

....

....

....

....

....

SERMON NOTES

Title: ....

Scripture: ....

Topics and Chains: ....

....

....

Main Topic: ....

Main Verses: ....

Main Points: ....

....

....

Supporting Topic: ....

Verses: ....

Points: ....

....

....

Supporting Topic: ....

Verses: ....

Points: ....

....

....

Additional Thoughts: ....

....

....

....

SERMON OUTLINE/NOTES

Title and Reference: ....

....

....

....

....

....

....

....

....

....

....

....

....

....

....

....

....

....

....

....

....

....

....

....

....

....

....

....

....

....

....

....

....

....

....

....

Sermon Notes

Title: ....

Scripture: ....

Topics and Chains: ....

....

....

....

Main Topic: ....

Main Verses: ....

....

Main Points: ....

....

....

....

Supporting Topic: ....

Verses: ....

....

Points: ....

....

....

....

Supporting Topic: ....

Verses: ....

....

Points: ....

....

....

....

Additional Thoughts: ....

....

....

....

....

SERMON OUTLINE/NOTES

Title and Reference: ....

....

....

....

....

....

....

....

....

....

....

....

....

....

....

....

....

....

....

....

....

....

....

....

....

....

....

....

....

....

....

....

....

SERMON NOTES

Title: ....

Scripture: ....

Topics and Chains: ....

....

....

....

Main Topic: ....

Main Verses: ....

....

Main Points: ....

....

....

....

Supporting Topic: ....

Verses: ....

....

Points: ....

....

....

....

Supporting Topic: ....

Verses: ....

....

Points: ....

....

....

....

Additional Thoughts: ....

....

....

....

....

SERMON OUTLINE/NOTES

Title and Reference: ....

....

....

....

....

....

....

....

....

....

....

....

....

....

....

....

....

....

....

....

....

....

....

....

....

....

....

....

....

....

....

....

....

....

....

SERMON NOTES

Title: ....

Scripture: ....

Topics and Chains: ....

....

....

....

Main Topic: ....

Main Verses: ....

....

Main Points: ....

....

....

....

Supporting Topic: ....

Verses: ....

....

Points: ....

....

....

....

Supporting Topic: ....

Verses: ....

....

Points: ....

....

....

....

Additional Thoughts: ....

....

....

....

....

SERMON OUTLINE/NOTES

Title and Reference: ....
....
....
....
....
....
....
....
....
....
....
....
....
....
....
....
....
....
....
....
....
....
....
....
....
....
....
....
....
....
....
....
....

SERMON NOTES

Title: ....

Scripture: ....

Topics and Chains: ....

....

....

....

Main Topic: ....

Main Verses: ....

....

Main Points: ....

....

....

....

Supporting Topic: ....

Verses: ....

....

Points: ....

....

....

....

Supporting Topic: ....

Verses: ....

....

Points: ....

....

....

....

Additional Thoughts: ....

....

....

....

SERMON OUTLINE/NOTES

Title and Reference: ....

....

....

....

....

....

....

....

....

....

....

....

....

....

....

....

....

....

....

....

....

....

....

....

....

....

....

....

....

....

....

SERMON NOTES

Title: ....

Scripture: ....

Topics and Chains: ....

....

....

....

Main Topic: ....

Main Verses: ....

....

Main Points: ....

....

....

....

Supporting Topic: ....

Verses: ....

....

Points: ....

....

....

....

Supporting Topic: ....

Verses: ....

....

Points: ....

....

....

....

Additional Thoughts: ....

....

....

....

SERMON OUTLINE/NOTES

Title and Reference: ....

....

....

....

....

....

....

....

....

....

....

....

....

....

....

....

....

....

....

....

....

....

....

....

....

....

....

....

....

....

....

....

....

SERMON NOTES

Title: ....

Scripture: ....

Topics and Chains: ....

....

....

....

Main Topic: ....

Main Verses: ....

....

Main Points: ....

....

....

....

Supporting Topic: ....

Verses: ....

....

Points: ....

....

....

....

Supporting Topic: ....

Verses: ....

....

Points: ....

....

....

....

Additional Thoughts: ....

....

....

....

....

SERMON OUTLINE/NOTES

Title and Reference: ....

....

....

....

....

....

....

....

....

....

....

....

....

....

....

....

....

....

....

....

....

....

....

....

....

....

....

....

....

....

....

....

....

....

....

Sermon Notes

Title: ....

Scripture: ....

Topics and Chains: ....

....

....

....

Main Topic: ....

Main Verses: ....

....

Main Points: ....

....

....

....

Supporting Topic: ....

Verses: ....

....

Points: ....

....

....

....

Supporting Topic: ....

Verses: ....

....

Points: ....

....

....

....

Additional Thoughts: ....

....

....

....

....

Sermon Outline/Notes

Title and Reference: ....

....

....

....

....

....

....

....

....

....

....

....

....

....

....

....

....

....

....

....

....

....

....

....

....

....

....

....

....

....

....

SERMON NOTES

Title: ....

Scripture: ....

Topics and Chains: ....

....

....

....

Main Topic: ....

Main Verses: ....

....

Main Points: ....

....

....

....

Supporting Topic: ....

Verses: ....

....

Points: ....

....

....

....

Supporting Topic: ....

Verses: ....

....

Points: ....

....

....

....

Additional Thoughts: ....

....

....

....

....

SERMON OUTLINE/NOTES

Title and Reference: ....

....

....

....

....

....

....

....

....

....

....

....

....

....

....

....

....

....

....

....

....

....

....

....

....

....

....

....

....

....

....

Sermon Notes

Title: ....

Scripture: ....

Topics and Chains: ....

....

....

....

Main Topic: ....

Main Verses: ....

....

Main Points: ....

....

....

....

Supporting Topic: ....

Verses: ....

....

Points: ....

....

....

....

Supporting Topic: ....

Verses: ....

....

Points: ....

....

....

....

Additional Thoughts: ....

....

....

....

....

SERMON OUTLINE/NOTES

Title and Reference: ....

....

....

....

....

....

....

....

....

....

....

....

....

....

....

....

....

....

....

....

....

....

....

....

....

....

....

....

....

....

....

....

....

SERMON NOTES

Title: ....

Scripture: ....

Topics and Chains: ....

....

....

....

Main Topic: ....

Main Verses: ....

....

Main Points: ....

....

....

....

Supporting Topic: ....

Verses: ....

....

Points: ....

....

....

....

Supporting Topic: ....

Verses: ....

....

Points: ....

....

....

....

Additional Thoughts: ....

....

....

....

....

SERMON OUTLINE/NOTES

Title and Reference: ....

....

....

....

....

....

....

....

....

....

....

....

....

....

....

....

....

....

....

....

....

....

....

....

....

....

....

....

....

....

....

....

....

....

....

SERMON NOTES

Title: ....

Scripture: ....

Topics and Chains: ....

....

....

Main Topic: ....

Main Verses: ....

Main Points: ....

....

....

Supporting Topic: ....

Verses: ....

Points: ....

....

....

Supporting Topic: ....

Verses: ....

Points: ....

....

....

Additional Thoughts: ....

....

....

....

....

Sermon Outline/Notes

Title and Reference: ....

....

....

....

....

....

....

....

....

....

....

....

....

....

....

....

....

....

....

....

....

....

....

....

....

....

....

....

....

....

....

....

SERMON NOTES

Title: ....

Scripture: ....

Topics and Chains: ....

....

....

....

Main Topic: ....

Main Verses: ....

....

Main Points: ....

....

....

....

Supporting Topic: ....

Verses: ....

....

Points: ....

....

....

....

Supporting Topic: ....

Verses: ....

....

Points: ....

....

....

....

Additional Thoughts: ....

....

....

....

....

SERMON OUTLINE/NOTES

Title and Reference: ....

....

....

....

....

....

....

....

....

....

....

....

....

....

....

....

....

....

....

....

....

....

....

....

....

....

....

....

....

....

SERMON NOTES

Title: ....

Scripture: ....

Topics and Chains: ....

....

....

....

Main Topic: ....

Main Verses: ....

....

Main Points: ....

....

....

....

Supporting Topic: ....

Verses: ....

....

Points: ....

....

....

....

Supporting Topic: ....

Verses: ....

....

Points: ....

....

....

....

Additional Thoughts: ....

....

....

....

....

SERMON OUTLINE/NOTES

Title and Reference: ....

SERMON NOTES

Title: ....

Scripture: ....

Topics and Chains: ....

....

....

....

Main Topic: ....

Main Verses: ....

....

Main Points: ....

....

....

....

Supporting Topic: ....

Verses: ....

....

Points: ....

....

....

....

Supporting Topic: ....

Verses: ....

....

Points: ....

....

....

....

Additional Thoughts: ....

....

....

....

....

SERMON OUTLINE/NOTES

Title and Reference: ....

....

....

....

....

....

....

....

....

....

....

....

....

....

....

....

....

....

....

....

....

....

....

....

....

....

....

....

....

....

....

....

Sermon Notes

Title: ....

Scripture: ....

Topics and Chains: ....

....

....

....

Main Topic: ....

Main Verses: ....

....

Main Points: ....

....

....

....

Supporting Topic: ....

Verses: ....

....

Points: ....

....

....

....

Supporting Topic: ....

Verses: ....

....

Points: ....

....

....

....

Additional Thoughts: ....

....

....

....

....

Sermon Outline/Notes

Title and Reference: ....
....
....
....
....
....
....
....
....
....
....
....
....
....
....
....
....
....
....
....
....
....
....
....
....
....
....
....
....
....
....
....
....

SERMON NOTES

Title: ....

Scripture: ....

Topics and Chains: ....

....

....

....

Main Topic: ....

Main Verses: ....

....

Main Points: ....

....

....

....

Supporting Topic: ....

Verses: ....

....

Points: ....

....

....

....

Supporting Topic: ....

Verses: ....

....

Points: ....

....

....

....

Additional Thoughts: ....

....

....

....

SERMON OUTLINE/NOTES

Title and Reference: ....

....

....

....

....

....

....

....

....

....

....

....

....

....

....

....

....

....

....

....

....

....

....

....

....

....

....

....

....

....

....

....

....

....

SERMON NOTES

Title: ....

Scripture: ....

Topics and Chains: ....

....

....

....

Main Topic: ....

Main Verses: ....

....

Main Points: ....

....

....

....

Supporting Topic: ....

Verses: ....

....

Points: ....

....

....

....

Supporting Topic: ....

Verses: ....

....

Points: ....

....

....

....

Additional Thoughts: ....

....

....

....

....

SERMON OUTLINE/NOTES

Title and Reference: ....

....

....

....

....

....

....

....

....

....

....

....

....

....

....

....

....

....

....

....

....

....

....

....

....

....

....

....

....

....

SERMON NOTES

Title: ....

Scripture: ....

Topics and Chains: ....

....

....

....

Main Topic: ....

Main Verses: ....

....

Main Points: ....

....

....

....

Supporting Topic: ....

Verses: ....

....

Points: ....

....

....

....

Supporting Topic: ....

Verses: ....

....

Points: ....

....

....

....

Additional Thoughts: ....

....

....

....

....

Sermon Outline/Notes

Title and Reference: ....

....

....

....

....

....

....

....

....

....

....

....

....

....

....

....

....

....

....

....

....

....

....

....

....

....

....

....

....

....

....

....

....

....

....

....

....

....

SERMON NOTES

Title: ....

Scripture: ....

Topics and Chains: ....

....

....

....

Main Topic: ....

Main Verses: ....

....

Main Points: ....

....

....

....

Supporting Topic: ....

Verses: ....

....

Points: ....

....

....

....

Supporting Topic: ....

Verses: ....

....

Points: ....

....

....

....

Additional Thoughts: ....

....

....

....

....

SERMON OUTLINE/NOTES

Title and Reference: ....

....

....

....

....

....

....

....

....

....

....

....

....

....

....

....

....

....

....

....

....

....

....

....

....

....

....

....

....

....

....

....

....

....

Sermon Notes

Title: ....

Scripture: ....

Topics and Chains: ....

....

....

....

Main Topic: ....

Main Verses: ....

....

Main Points: ....

....

....

....

Supporting Topic: ....

Verses: ....

....

Points: ....

....

....

....

Supporting Topic: ....

Verses: ....

....

Points: ....

....

....

....

Additional Thoughts: ....

....

....

....

....

SERMON OUTLINE/NOTES

Title and Reference: ....

....

....

....

....

....

....

....

....

....

....

....

....

....

....

....

....

....

....

....

....

....

....

....

....

....

....

....

....

....

....

....

....

....

....

....

....

....

SERMON NOTES

Title: ....

Scripture: ....

Topics and Chains: ....
....
....
....

Main Topic: ....

Main Verses: ....
....

Main Points: ....
....
....
....

Supporting Topic: ....

Verses: ....
....

Points: ....
....
....
....

Supporting Topic: ....

Verses: ....
....

Points: ....
....
....
....

Additional Thoughts: ....
....
....
....
....

SERMON OUTLINE/NOTES

Title and Reference: ....

....

....

....

....

....

....

....

....

....

....

....

....

....

....

....

....

....

....

....

....

....

....

....

....

....

....

....

....

....

SERMON NOTES

Title: ....

Scripture: ....

Topics and Chains: ....

....

....

....

Main Topic: ....

Main Verses: ....

....

Main Points: ....

....

....

....

Supporting Topic: ....

Verses: ....

....

Points: ....

....

....

....

Supporting Topic: ....

Verses: ....

....

Points: ....

....

....

....

Additional Thoughts: ....

....

....

....

SERMON OUTLINE/NOTES

Title and Reference: ....

....

....

....

....

....

....

....

....

....

....

....

....

....

....

....

....

....

....

....

....

....

....

....

....

....

....

....

....

....

SERMON NOTES

Title: ....

Scripture: ....

Topics and Chains: ....

....

....

Main Topic: ....

Main Verses: ....

....

Main Points: ....

....

....

....

Supporting Topic: ....

Verses: ....

....

Points: ....

....

....

....

Supporting Topic: ....

Verses: ....

....

Points: ....

....

....

....

Additional Thoughts: ....

....

....

....

....

SERMON OUTLINE/NOTES

Title and Reference: ....

....

....

....

....

....

....

....

....

....

....

....

....

....

....

....

....

....

....

....

....

....

....

....

....

....

....

....

....

....

....

....

SERMON NOTES

Title: ....

Scripture: ....

Topics and Chains: ....

....

....

....

Main Topic: ....

Main Verses: ....

....

Main Points: ....

....

....

....

Supporting Topic: ....

Verses: ....

....

Points: ....

....

....

....

Supporting Topic: ....

Verses: ....

....

Points: ....

....

....

....

Additional Thoughts: ....

....

....

....

....

SERMON OUTLINE/NOTES

Title and Reference: ....
....
....
....
....
....
....
....
....
....
....
....
....
....
....
....
....
....
....
....
....
....
....
....
....
....
....
....
....
....
....
....
....
....
....

SERMON NOTES

Title: ....

Scripture: ....

Topics and Chains: ....

....

....

....

Main Topic: ....

Main Verses: ....

....

Main Points: ....

....

....

....

Supporting Topic: ....

Verses: ....

....

Points: ....

....

....

....

Supporting Topic: ....

Verses: ....

....

Points: ....

....

....

....

Additional Thoughts: ....

....

....

....

....

SERMON OUTLINE/NOTES

Title and Reference: ....
....
....
....
....
....
....
....
....
....
....
....
....
....
....
....
....
....
....
....
....
....
....
....
....
....
....
....
....
....
....
....
....

SERMON NOTES

Title: ....

Scripture: ....

Topics and Chains: ....

....

....

....

Main Topic: ....

Main Verses: ....

Main Points: ....

....

....

....

Supporting Topic: ....

Verses: ....

....

Points: ....

....

....

....

Supporting Topic: ....

Verses: ....

....

Points: ....

....

....

....

Additional Thoughts: ....

....

....

....

....

Sermon Outline/Notes

Title and Reference: ....

....

....

....

....

....

....

....

....

....

....

....

....

....

....

....

....

....

....

....

....

....

....

....

....

....

....

....

....

....

....

....

....

SERMON NOTES

Title: ....

Scripture: ....

Topics and Chains: ....

....

....

....

Main Topic: ....

Main Verses: ....

....

Main Points: ....

....

....

....

Supporting Topic: ....

Verses: ....

....

Points: ....

....

....

....

Supporting Topic: ....

Verses: ....

....

Points: ....

....

....

....

Additional Thoughts: ....

....

....

....

....

SERMON OUTLINE/NOTES

Title and Reference: ....

SERMON NOTES

Title: ....

Scripture: ....

Topics and Chains: ....

....

....

Main Topic: ....

Main Verses: ....

....

Main Points: ....

....

....

....

Supporting Topic: ....

Verses: ....

....

Points: ....

....

....

....

Supporting Topic: ....

Verses: ....

....

Points: ....

....

....

....

Additional Thoughts: ....

....

....

....

....

SERMON OUTLINE/NOTES

Title and Reference: ....

....

....

....

....

....

....

....

....

....

....

....

....

....

....

....

....

....

....

....

....

....

....

....

....

....

....

....

....

....

....

....

....

....

SERMON NOTES

Title: ....

Scripture: ....

Topics and Chains: ....

....

....

....

Main Topic: ....

Main Verses: ....

....

Main Points: ....

....

....

....

Supporting Topic: ....

Verses: ....

....

Points: ....

....

....

....

Supporting Topic: ....

Verses: ....

....

Points: ....

....

....

....

Additional Thoughts: ....

....

....

....

....

SERMON OUTLINE/NOTES

Title and Reference: ....

....

....

....

....

....

....

....

....

....

....

....

....

....

....

....

....

....

....

....

....

....

....

....

....

....

....

....

....

....

....

....

....

SERMON NOTES

Title: ....

Scripture: ....

Topics and Chains: ....

....

....

....

Main Topic: ....

Main Verses: ....

....

Main Points: ....

....

....

....

Supporting Topic: ....

Verses: ....

....

Points: ....

....

....

....

Supporting Topic: ....

Verses: ....

....

Points: ....

....

....

....

Additional Thoughts: ....

....

....

....

....

Sermon Outline/Notes

Title and Reference: ....

....

....

....

....

....

....

....

....

....

....

....

....

....

....

....

....

....

....

....

....

....

....

....

....

....

....

....

....

....

SERMON NOTES

Title: ....

Scripture: ....

Topics and Chains: ....

....

....

....

Main Topic: ....

Main Verses: ....

....

Main Points: ....

....

....

....

Supporting Topic: ....

Verses: ....

....

Points: ....

....

....

....

Supporting Topic: ....

Verses: ....

....

Points: ....

....

....

....

Additional Thoughts: ....

....

....

....

....

SERMON OUTLINE/NOTES

Title and Reference:

SERMON NOTES

Title: ....

Scripture: ....

Topics and Chains: ....

....

....

....

Main Topic: ....

Main Verses: ....

....

Main Points: ....

....

....

....

Supporting Topic: ....

Verses: ....

....

Points: ....

....

....

....

Supporting Topic: ....

Verses: ....

....

Points: ....

....

....

....

Additional Thoughts: ....

....

....

....

....

SERMON OUTLINE/NOTES

Title and Reference: ....

....

....

....

....

....

....

....

....

....

....

....

....

....

....

....

....

....

....

....

....

....

....

....

....

....

....

....

....

SERMON NOTES

Title: ....

Scripture: ....

Topics and Chains: ....

....

....

....

Main Topic: ....

Main Verses: ....

Main Points: ....

....

....

....

Supporting Topic: ....

Verses: ....

....

Points: ....

....

....

....

Supporting Topic: ....

Verses: ....

....

Points: ....

....

....

....

Additional Thoughts: ....

....

....

....

....

SERMON OUTLINE/NOTES

Title and Reference: ....

....

....

....

....

....

....

....

....

....

....

....

....

....

....

....

....

....

....

....

....

....

....

....

....

....

....

....

....

....

....

....

....

....

Sermon Notes

Title: ....

Scripture: ....

Topics and Chains: ....

....

....

....

Main Topic: ....

Main Verses: ....

....

Main Points: ....

....

....

....

Supporting Topic: ....

Verses: ....

....

Points: ....

....

....

....

Supporting Topic: ....

Verses: ....

....

Points: ....

....

....

....

Additional Thoughts: ....

....

....

....

....

SERMON OUTLINE/NOTES

Title and Reference: ....

....

....

....

....

....

....

....

....

....

....

....

....

....

....

....

....

....

....

....

....

....

....

....

....

....

....

....

....

....

....

....

SERMON NOTES

Title: ....

Scripture: ....

Topics and Chains: ....

....

....

....

Main Topic: ....

Main Verses: ....

....

Main Points: ....

....

....

....

Supporting Topic: ....

Verses: ....

....

Points: ....

....

....

....

Supporting Topic: ....

Verses: ....

....

Points: ....

....

....

....

Additional Thoughts: ....

....

....

....

....

SERMON OUTLINE/NOTES

Title and Reference: ....

....

....

....

....

....

....

....

....

....

....

....

....

....

....

....

....

....

....

....

....

....

....

....

....

....

....

....

....

....

....

....

SERMON NOTES

Title: ....

Scripture: ....

Topics and Chains: ....

....

....

....

Main Topic: ....

Main Verses: ....

....

Main Points: ....

....

....

....

Supporting Topic: ....

Verses: ....

....

Points: ....

....

....

Supporting Topic: ....

Verses: ....

....

Points: ....

....

....

Additional Thoughts: ....

....

....

....

Sermon Outline/Notes

Title and Reference: ....

....

....

....

....

....

....

....

....

....

....

....

....

....

....

....

....

....

....

....

....

....

....

....

....

....

....

....

....

....

....

....

SERMON NOTES

Title: ....

Scripture: ....

Topics and Chains: ....

....

....

....

Main Topic: ....

Main Verses: ....

....

Main Points: ....

....

....

....

Supporting Topic: ....

Verses: ....

....

Points: ....

....

....

....

Supporting Topic: ....

Verses: ....

....

Points: ....

....

....

....

Additional Thoughts: ....

....

....

....

....

SERMON OUTLINE/NOTES

Title and Reference: ....

....

....

....

....

....

....

....

....

....

....

....

....

....

....

....

....

....

....

....

....

....

....

....

....

....

....

....

....

....

....

....

....

....

....

SERMON NOTES

Title: ....

Scripture: ....

Topics and Chains: ....

....

....

Main Topic: ....

Main Verses: ....

Main Points: ....

....

....

Supporting Topic: ....

Verses: ....

Points: ....

....

....

Supporting Topic: ....

Verses: ....

Points: ....

....

....

Additional Thoughts: ....

....

....

....

SERMON OUTLINE/NOTES

Title and Reference: ....

....

....

....

....

....

....

....

....

....

....

....

....

....

....

....

....

....

....

....

....

....

....

....

....

....

....

....

....

....

....

SERMON NOTES

Title: ....

Scripture: ....

Topics and Chains: ....

....

....

....

Main Topic: ....

Main Verses: ....

....

Main Points: ....

....

....

....

Supporting Topic: ....

Verses: ....

....

Points: ....

....

....

....

Supporting Topic: ....

Verses: ....

....

Points: ....

....

....

....

Additional Thoughts: ....

....

....

....

....

SERMON OUTLINE/NOTES

Title and Reference: ....

....
....
....
....
....
....
....
....
....
....
....
....
....
....
....
....
....
....
....
....
....
....
....
....
....
....
....
....
....
....
....
....
....
....
....

Sermon Notes

Title: ....
Scripture: ....
Topics and Chains: ....
....
....
....

Main Topic: ....
Main Verses: ....
....
Main Points: ....
....
....
....

Supporting Topic: ....
Verses: ....
....
Points: ....
....
....
....

Supporting Topic: ....
Verses: ....
....
Points: ....
....
....
....

Additional Thoughts: ....
....
....
....
....

SERMON OUTLINE/NOTES

Title and Reference: ....

....

....

....

....

....

....

....

....

....

....

....

....

....

....

....

....

....

....

....

....

....

....

....

....

....

....

....

....

SERMON NOTES

Title: ....

Scripture: ....

Topics and Chains: ....

....

....

....

Main Topic: ....

Main Verses: ....

....

Main Points: ....

....

....

....

Supporting Topic: ....

Verses: ....

....

Points: ....

....

....

....

Supporting Topic: ....

Verses: ....

....

Points: ....

....

....

....

Additional Thoughts: ....

....

....

....

....

SERMON OUTLINE/NOTES

Title and Reference: ....

....

....

....

....

....

....

....

....

....

....

....

....

....

....

....

....

....

....

....

....

....

....

....

....

....

....

....

....

....

....

....

....

Sermon Notes

Title: ....

Scripture: ....

Topics and Chains: ....

....

....

....

Main Topic: ....

Main Verses: ....

....

Main Points: ....

....

....

....

Supporting Topic: ....

Verses: ....

....

Points: ....

....

....

....

Supporting Topic: ....

Verses: ....

....

Points: ....

....

....

....

Additional Thoughts: ....

....

....

....

....

Sermon Outline/Notes

Title and Reference: ....

....

....

....

....

....

....

....

....

....

....

....

....

....

....

....

....

....

....

....

....

....

....

....

....

....

....

....

....

....

....

....

....

....

SERMON NOTES

Title: ....

Scripture: ....

Topics and Chains: ....

....

....

....

Main Topic: ....

Main Verses: ....

....

Main Points: ....

....

....

....

Supporting Topic: ....

Verses: ....

....

Points: ....

....

....

....

Supporting Topic: ....

Verses: ....

....

Points: ....

....

....

....

Additional Thoughts: ....

....

....

....

Sermon Outline/Notes

Title and Reference: ....

....

....

....

....

....

....

....

....

....

....

....

....

....

....

....

....

....

....

....

....

....

....

....

....

....

....

....

....

....

....

....

Sermon Notes

Title: ....

Scripture: ....

Topics and Chains: ....

....

....

....

Main Topic: ....

Main Verses: ....

....

Main Points: ....

....

....

....

Supporting Topic: ....

Verses: ....

....

Points: ....

....

....

....

Supporting Topic: ....

Verses: ....

....

Points: ....

....

....

....

Additional Thoughts: ....

....

....

....

....

SERMON OUTLINE/NOTES

Title and Reference: ....

....

....

....

....

....

....

....

....

....

....

....

....

....

....

....

....

....

....

....

....

....

....

....

....

....

....

....

....

....

....

....

....

....

SERMON NOTES

Title: ....

Scripture: ....

Topics and Chains: ....

....

....

....

Main Topic: ....

Main Verses: ....

....

Main Points: ....

....

....

....

Supporting Topic: ....

Verses: ....

....

Points: ....

....

....

....

Supporting Topic: ....

Verses: ....

....

Points: ....

....

....

....

Additional Thoughts: ....

....

....

....

....

SERMON OUTLINE/NOTES

Title and Reference: ....

....

....

....

....

....

....

....

....

....

....

....

....

....

....

....

....

....

....

....

....

....

....

....

....

....

....

....

....

....

....

....

SERMON NOTES

Title: ....

Scripture: ....

Topics and Chains: ....

....

....

....

Main Topic: ....

Main Verses: ....

....

Main Points: ....

....

....

....

Supporting Topic: ....

Verses: ....

....

Points: ....

....

....

....

Supporting Topic: ....

Verses: ....

....

Points: ....

....

....

....

Additional Thoughts: ....

....

....

....

....

SERMON OUTLINE/NOTES

Title and Reference: ....

....

....

....

....

....

....

....

....

....

....

....

....

....

....

....

....

....

....

....

....

....

....

....

....

....

....

....

....

....

....

....

....

SERMON NOTES

Title: ....

Scripture: ....

Topics and Chains: ....

....

....

....

Main Topic: ....

Main Verses: ....

....

Main Points: ....

....

....

....

Supporting Topic: ....

Verses: ....

....

Points: ....

....

....

....

Supporting Topic: ....

Verses: ....

....

Points: ....

....

....

....

Additional Thoughts: ....

....

....

....

....

Sermon Outline/Notes

Title and Reference: ....

....

....

....

....

....

....

....

....

....

....

....

....

....

....

....

....

....

....

....

....

....

....

....

....

....

....

....

....

....

....

....

....

....

....

Sermon Notes

Title: ....

Scripture: ....

Topics and Chains: ....

....

....

....

Main Topic: ....

Main Verses: ....

....

Main Points: ....

....

....

....

Supporting Topic: ....

Verses: ....

....

Points: ....

....

....

....

Supporting Topic: ....

Verses: ....

....

Points: ....

....

....

....

Additional Thoughts: ....

....

....

....

....

SERMON OUTLINE/NOTES

Title and Reference: ....

SERMON NOTES

Title: ....

Scripture: ....

Topics and Chains: ....

....

....

....

Main Topic: ....

Main Verses: ....

....

Main Points: ....

....

....

....

Supporting Topic: ....

Verses: ....

....

Points: ....

....

....

....

Supporting Topic: ....

Verses: ....

....

Points: ....

....

....

....

Additional Thoughts: ....

....

....

....

....

SERMON OUTLINE/NOTES

Title and Reference: ....

Sermon Notes

Title: ....

Scripture: ....

Topics and Chains: ....

....

....

....

Main Topic: ....

Main Verses: ....

Main Points: ....

....

....

....

Supporting Topic: ....

Verses: ....

....

Points: ....

....

....

....

Supporting Topic: ....

Verses: ....

....

Points: ....

....

....

....

Additional Thoughts: ....

....

....

....

....

Sermon Outline/Notes

Title and Reference: ....

....

....

....

....

....

....

....

....

....

....

....

....

....

....

....

....

....

....

....

....

....

....

....

....

....

....

....

....

....

....

....

....

....

....

....

SERMON NOTES

Title: ....

Scripture: ....

Topics and Chains: ....

....

....

....

Main Topic: ....

Main Verses: ....

....

Main Points: ....

....

....

....

Supporting Topic: ....

Verses: ....

....

Points: ....

....

....

....

Supporting Topic: ....

Verses: ....

....

Points: ....

....

....

....

Additional Thoughts: ....

....

....

....

....

Sermon Outline/Notes

Title and Reference: ....

....

....

....

....

....

....

....

....

....

....

....

....

....

....

....

....

....

....

....

....

....

....

....

....

....

....

....

....

....

....

SERMON NOTES

Title: ....

Scripture: ....

Topics and Chains: ....

....

....

Main Topic: ....

Main Verses: ....

....

Main Points: ....

....

....

Supporting Topic: ....

Verses: ....

....

Points: ....

....

....

Supporting Topic: ....

Verses: ....

....

Points: ....

....

....

Additional Thoughts: ....

....

....

....

....

SERMON OUTLINE/NOTES

Title and Reference: ....

....

....

....

....

....

....

....

....

....

....

....

....

....

....

....

....

....

....

....

....

....

....

....

....

....

....

....

....

....

....

....

....

....

Sermon Notes

Title: ....

Scripture: ....

Topics and Chains: ....

....

....

....

Main Topic: ....

Main Verses: ....

....

Main Points: ....

....

....

....

Supporting Topic: ....

Verses: ....

....

Points: ....

....

....

....

Supporting Topic: ....

Verses: ....

....

Points: ....

....

....

....

Additional Thoughts: ....

....

....

....

....

SERMON OUTLINE/NOTES

Title and Reference: ....

....

....

....

....

....

....

....

....

....

....

....

....

....

....

....

....

....

....

....

....

....

....

....

....

....

....

....

....

....

....

....

....

SERMON NOTES

Title: ....

Scripture: ....

Topics and Chains: ....

....

....

....

Main Topic: ....

Main Verses: ....

....

Main Points: ....

....

....

....

Supporting Topic: ....

Verses: ....

....

Points: ....

....

....

....

Supporting Topic: ....

Verses: ....

....

Points: ....

....

....

....

Additional Thoughts: ....

....

....

....

....

SERMON OUTLINE/NOTES

Title and Reference: ....

....

....

....

....

....

....

....

....

....

....

....

....

....

....

....

....

....

....

....

....

....

....

....

....

....

....

....

....

....

....

....

....

SERMON NOTES

Title: ....

Scripture: ....

Topics and Chains: ....

....

....

....

Main Topic: ....

Main Verses: ....

....

Main Points: ....

....

....

....

Supporting Topic: ....

Verses: ....

....

Points: ....

....

....

....

Supporting Topic: ....

Verses: ....

....

Points: ....

....

....

....

Additional Thoughts: ....

....

....

....

....

SERMON OUTLINE/NOTES

Title and Reference: ....

Sermon Notes

Title: ....

Scripture: ....

Topics and Chains: ....

....

....

....

Main Topic: ....

Main Verses: ....

Main Points: ....

....

....

....

Supporting Topic: ....

Verses: ....

....

Points: ....

....

....

....

Supporting Topic: ....

Verses: ....

....

Points: ....

....

....

....

Additional Thoughts: ....

....

....

....

....

Sermon Outline/Notes

Title and Reference: ....

....

....

....

....

....

....

....

....

....

....

....

....

....

....

....

....

....

....

....

....

....

....

....

....

....

....

....

....

....

....

....

....

SERMON NOTES

Title: ....

Scripture: ....

Topics and Chains: ....

....

....

Main Topic: ....

Main Verses: ....

....

Main Points: ....

....

....

Supporting Topic: ....

Verses: ....

....

Points: ....

....

....

Supporting Topic: ....

Verses: ....

....

Points: ....

....

....

Additional Thoughts: ....

....

....

....

....

SERMON OUTLINE/NOTES

Title and Reference: ....

....

....

....

....

....

....

....

....

....

....

....

....

....

....

....

....

....

....

....

....

....

....

....

....

....

....

....

....

....

....

SERMON NOTES

Title: ....

Scripture: ....

Topics and Chains: ....

....

....

....

Main Topic: ....

Main Verses: ....

....

Main Points: ....

....

....

Supporting Topic: ....

Verses: ....

....

Points: ....

....

....

Supporting Topic: ....

Verses: ....

....

Points: ....

....

....

Additional Thoughts: ....

....

....

....

SERMON OUTLINE/NOTES

Title and Reference: ....

....

....

....

....

....

....

....

....

....

....

....

....

....

....

....

....

....

....

....

....

....

....

....

....

....

....

....

....

....

....

....

....

....

....

....

....

SERMON NOTES

Title: ....

Scripture: ....

Topics and Chains: ....

....

....

....

Main Topic: ....

Main Verses: ....

....

Main Points: ....

....

....

....

Supporting Topic: ....

Verses: ....

....

Points: ....

....

....

....

Supporting Topic: ....

Verses: ....

....

Points: ....

....

....

....

Additional Thoughts: ....

....

....

....

SERMON OUTLINE/NOTES

Title and Reference: ....

....

....

....

....

....

....

....

....

....

....

....

....

....

....

....

....

....

....

....

....

....

....

....

....

....

....

....

....

....

....

SERMON NOTES

Title: ....

Scripture: ....

Topics and Chains: ....

....

....

....

Main Topic: ....

Main Verses: ....

....

Main Points: ....

....

....

....

Supporting Topic: ....

Verses: ....

....

Points: ....

....

....

....

Supporting Topic: ....

Verses: ....

....

Points: ....

....

....

....

Additional Thoughts: ....

....

....

....

....

SERMON OUTLINE/NOTES

Title and Reference: ....

....

....

....

....

....

....

....

....

....

....

....

....

....

....

....

....

....

....

....

....

....

....

....

....

....

....

....

....

....

....

....

....

....

....

SERMON NOTES

Title: ....

Scripture: ....

Topics and Chains: ....

....

....

Main Topic: ....

Main Verses: ....

Main Points: ....

....

....

Supporting Topic: ....

Verses: ....

....

Points: ....

....

....

Supporting Topic: ....

Verses: ....

....

Points: ....

....

....

Additional Thoughts: ....

....

....

....

....

Sermon Outline/Notes

Title and Reference: ....

....

....

....

....

....

....

....

....

....

....

....

....

....

....

....

....

....

....

....

....

....

....

....

....

....

....

....

....

....

....

....

....

Sermon Notes

Title: ....

Scripture: ....

Topics and Chains: ....

....

....

....

Main Topic: ....

Main Verses: ....

Main Points: ....

....

....

....

Supporting Topic: ....

Verses: ....

Points: ....

....

....

....

Supporting Topic: ....

Verses: ....

Points: ....

....

....

....

Additional Thoughts: ....

....

....

....

....

SERMON OUTLINE/NOTES

Title and Reference: ....

....

....

....

....

....

....

....

....

....

....

....

....

....

....

....

....

....

....

....

....

....

....

....

....

....

....

....

....

....

....

....

SERMON NOTES

Title: ....

Scripture: ....

Topics and Chains: ....

....

....

....

Main Topic: ....

Main Verses: ....

....

Main Points: ....

....

....

....

Supporting Topic: ....

Verses: ....

....

Points: ....

....

....

....

Supporting Topic: ....

Verses: ....

....

Points: ....

....

....

....

Additional Thoughts: ....

....

....

....

SERMON OUTLINE/NOTES

Title and Reference: ....

....

....

....

....

....

....

....

....

....

....

....

....

....

....

....

....

....

....

....

....

....

....

....

....

....

....

....

....

....

....

....

....

....

....

Sermon Notes

Title: ....

Scripture: ....

Topics and Chains: ....

....

....

....

Main Topic: ....

Main Verses: ....

....

Main Points: ....

....

....

....

Supporting Topic: ....

Verses: ....

....

Points: ....

....

....

....

Supporting Topic: ....

Verses: ....

....

Points: ....

....

....

....

Additional Thoughts: ....

....

....

....

....

Sermon Outline/Notes

Title and Reference: ....

....

....

....

....

....

....

....

....

....

....

....

....

....

....

....

....

....

....

....

....

....

....

....

....

....

....

....

....

....

....

SERMON NOTES

Title: ....

Scripture: ....

Topics and Chains: ....

....

....

....

Main Topic: ....

Main Verses: ....

....

Main Points: ....

....

....

....

Supporting Topic: ....

Verses: ....

....

Points: ....

....

....

....

Supporting Topic: ....

Verses: ....

....

Points: ....

....

....

....

Additional Thoughts: ....

....

....

....

....

SERMON OUTLINE/NOTES

Title and Reference: ....
....
....
....
....
....
....
....
....
....
....
....
....
....
....
....
....
....
....
....
....
....
....
....
....
....
....
....
....
....
....
....
....
....

Sermon Notes

Title: ....

Scripture: ....

Topics and Chains: ....

....

....

....

Main Topic: ....

Main Verses: ....

Main Points: ....

....

....

....

Supporting Topic: ....

Verses: ....

....

Points: ....

....

....

....

Supporting Topic: ....

Verses: ....

....

Points: ....

....

....

....

Additional Thoughts: ....

....

....

....

....

Sermon Outline/Notes

Title and Reference: ....

....

....

....

....

....

....

....

....

....

....

....

....

....

....

....

....

....

....

....

....

....

....

....

....

....

....

....

....

Sermon Notes

Title: ....

Scripture: ....

Topics and Chains: ....

....

....

....

Main Topic: ....

Main Verses: ....

....

Main Points: ....

....

....

....

Supporting Topic: ....

Verses: ....

....

Points: ....

....

....

....

Supporting Topic: ....

Verses: ....

....

Points: ....

....

....

....

Additional Thoughts: ....

....

....

....

Sermon Outline/Notes

Title and Reference: ....

....

....

....

....

....

....

....

....

....

....

....

....

....

....

....

....

....

....

....

....

....

....

....

....

....

....

....

SERMON NOTES

Title: ....

Scripture: ....

Topics and Chains: ....

....

....

....

Main Topic: ....

Main Verses: ....

....

Main Points: ....

....

....

....

Supporting Topic: ....

Verses: ....

....

Points: ....

....

....

....

Supporting Topic: ....

Verses: ....

....

Points: ....

....

....

....

Additional Thoughts: ....

....

....

....

....

SERMON OUTLINE/NOTES

Title and Reference: ....

....

....

....

....

....

....

....

....

....

....

....

....

....

....

....

....

....

....

....

....

....

....

....

....

....

....

....

....

....

....

....

....

....

SERMON INDEX

Sermon Index

....
....
....
....
....
....
....
....
....
....
....
....
....
....
....
....
....
....
....
....
....
....
....
....
....
....
....
....
....
....
....
....
....
....
....

SERMON INDEX
(CONTINUED)

Sermon Index

SERMON INDEX

(CONTINUED)

Sermon Index